THE 90-MINUTE EXIT STRATEGY

How To Get Your Exit Strategy Sorted In Just 90 Minutes...

Mark Westcott

Copyright © 2014 The Strategic Evolution
All rights reserved.
ISBN-10: 1495405206
ISBN-13: 978-1495405204

Here's What's Inside...

5 **Introduction**

7 **Why Don't More Business Owners Do Their Exit Strategy?**

8 **How Dan Sullivan's 80% Approach Changed My View of What's Possible...**

9 **Why Most People Fail to Have an Exit Plan in Place...**

13 **The 90 Minute Exit Strategy Works For Anyone...**

14 **What Happens When You Don't Have an Exit Strategy Sorted?**

18 **There are Many Reasons to Have an Exit Plan in Place...**

20 **Why Having a Lawyer or CPA Doesn't Mean Your Plan Is Sound...**

21 **The Different Types of Exit Plans...**

23 **The Only 3 Things You Need to Get Your Exit Plan in Place**

24 **Here's Exactly How The 90 Minute Exit Strategy Works...**

25 The 90 Minute Exit Strategy Can Give You Peace of Mind...

26 **The 90 Minute Exit Plan Works Even If You've Employed the Services of a CPA and Lawyer...**

29 **Here's Exactly How to Get Your Exit Plan in Place in Just 90 Minutes...**

Introduction

January 2014
Sanctuary Cove, Australia

One of the things I've come to realise over the years in working with business owners is there seems to almost be an inverse relationship between those that need to have an exit strategy in place and those that actually do.

In other words, business owners who spend most of their time growing and expanding their business are the ones who need an exit plan the most, but because they are often too busy working in their business they never find the time to step back and ask where is all this going? When and how do I want to get out of this business someday? And what happens if something unthinkable happens to me - what will my family be left with? A big mess to clean up or will I have everything sorted and in place, as it should be?

I see it all the time. The busier you are the more important the plan is, yet the least amount of time you seem to have to make for it. And the cycle persists.

Because of this, I knew I had to set out to make succession and estate planning simple for my clients. The time involvement had to fit with their busy lives.

This book is the result of that idea.

I created a structure to help people - plan, document and complete their legacy and succession plans in a short period of time and with very little effort by them - less time than it takes to sit through a movie in fact.

What follows is a conversation I had where I show you how to get yourself sorted and to make sure the legacy you wish to leave for your loved ones is achieved.

Kind regards,

Mark Westcott

The 90 Minute Exit Strategy

Susan: Hi everyone, this is Susan Austin and with me is Mark Westcott of Strategic Evolution out of Sanctuary Cove, Australia. Good morning Mark.

Mark: Hi Susan. This is great to be chatting with you this morning.

Susan: I'm glad you're here. We're going to be talking about your 90 Minute Exit Strategy. How to get your exit plan sorted and documented in just 90 minutes. Let's just jump right in. Why a 90 Minute Exit Strategy Mark?

Why Don't More Business Owners Do Their Exit Strategy?

Mark: That's a great question. I'll refer back to when I was at a conference of motor dealers last year. One of the things that resonated with me was that everybody seems to think that the exit planning and business succession planning, transition planning is all too hard. They just keep deferring it. They keep putting it off and think that they'll get to it one day but of course that day never comes. The main reason, which became obvious to me at that conference, was that people just think it's too hard to do. They get wound up in the complexity, in the jargon. Not knowing where or how to begin.

I've talked to their accountants, I've heard their lawyers talk about this and because there's so much complexity in actually putting together the clinical part of wills and succession plans and so on, they don't feel like they've got the time to allocate to it and other things become more urgent, other things become more pressing and so they keep deferring it. We refer to that as the deferral dilemma. People just keep putting off paying attention to it because of the energy and the time that they believe that they need to allocate to it.

What came from that, was what if we could simplify this for people? Speak in simple English with them and come up with some great questions to get to the essence of what people's intent is for their estate and business and to understand what people want to achieve? If you can get to that essence, the rest of the process is just clinical and it could be done by the professional advisors without the constant input of the client.

How Dan Sullivan's 80% Approach Changed My View of What's Possible...

Dan Sullivan of Strategic Coach has a theory he calls the 80% theory. This is just a perfect application of the 80% theory in regard to what's going on here.

The theory is, the most important 80% of executing their exit planning and their business succession and transition planning, is actually taking the first step and just getting the intent of people so that they can have a distilled understanding of what they want to achieve. Once you've got that, that's really 80% of the whole process - the understanding of what the person wants.

I'm saying, in 90 minutes, if you've got the right questions and you've got the right process, 90 minutes is all it takes to have an understanding from the client in regard to what they want to achieve. That was a light bulb moment and it's why I'm writing this book. To show people that it's a lot easier than they think.

Why Most People Fail to Have an Exit Plan in Place...

Susan: Very exciting Mark. For the business owner who's been putting this off for years and knows this should be addressed this has to be music to their ears. Tell me this, why is this such an issue for folks?

Mark: Research shows around 95% of exit and succession plans are either non-existent, (incomplete) or badly constructed. That's despite the best intentions of clients who have established relationships with their professional advisors. The real disadvantage of this is people then don't have a structured plan to direct their outcomes. We've done some research and on average the efficiency of most people's plans comes in at around just 18%. In other words, for most people there's a risk of only about

18% of what you intend to happen is documented in a way to ensure your intentions are carried out.

Frankly, we find that number way too low, so what we've tried to do is work out how to help people transition from the 18%. We work with our clients to get their legacy or transition efficiency to 100%. In other words, make the transition of your assets, the sale of your business or the family transition of your business, with the greatest ease and efficiency. The 90 Minute Exit Strategy is appropriate because in 90 minutes we can get from a client, with tailored questions, and a really sustained process that we've perfected, we can get that information from clients to improve the efficiency of what they're trying to achieve and as a result the effectiveness of what they're trying to achieve.

Susan: All this in less time than it takes to watch a movie Mark? You can work out their entire succession plan in less than 2 hours?

Mark: Absolutely. Movies go for about two to two and a half hours as it turns out. You're absolutely right. They can send the family off to watch a movie and we can sit down and do all their exit and succession planning and then off to dinner they go. This doesn't have to be the ordeal they think it is.

Susan: Did I understand you correctly earlier Mark? You said that statistically speaking only 18% of what people intend for their business, for their exit strategy, only 18% of their wants are being fulfilled? To turn that around, 80% of what people intend is not happening because it's not documented properly? Did I understand you correctly?

Mark: You did. The first statistic is even more concerning. 95% of people don't have a properly constructed exit plan. If you take that across the board, what people would want to happen on average only 18% of people's wants, their desires, their intent is truly the outcome. This is more easily measured for example when someone passes or dies because you can see what happens to their estates. Even in regard to transition planning of the business, succession planning of a business when everyone is still well and alive, what happens is people leave everything to the last minute.

They don't spend enough time before the event and the actual transition of the business between family members or to other partners in the business. There's a lot of inefficiency from either a taxation point of view or an effectiveness point of view. On average roughly 80% of what you want to happen isn't going to happen until you take the time to sit down and properly document it.

Susan: You're saying to document what someone wants to happen doesn't have to be this big ordeal we think it is in our minds. We have this vision that it's going to be agonizing and painful. In fact, you're making the point, I believe, that they don't have to understand all the ins and outs of estate planning - leave that to the professionals and so you've created this process and you've streamlined it so you get to the meat of what they want to happen in just 90 minutes. I love it. They essentially make the appointment with you and you handle the rest.

Mark: That's right. I've always craved simplicity for people and I think people have built this whole concept of exit planning into something that's a mountain that they can't possibly climb over. That's actually not true. If you attack it the right way, if you've got somebody with a structure and a process and great questions, as I said before, 80% of what needs to happen can happen in the 90 minutes. You just need people to actually sit still for up to 90 minutes and to discuss what they want to happen. What I like to do is to try and get into people's hearts and find out what people's real intent is. That's the most important part of the discovery.

What is it that they want for those that they care for? Those that they love? For the people that they have business relationships and so on? What is the ideal outcome? The intent and the ideal outcome to me are the most important things that I try to elicit from a conversation with a client. Once they actually talk about it and can articulate it to us, the mechanics aren't that difficult. What happens is people feel that they have to do everything in the process. They think they have to figure out HOW to do what they want to do and I'm here to tell them, no, they just need to tell us WHAT they want to happen.

I'm a great believer in another Strategic Coach concept called Unique Ability. We're all good at certain things. Traditionally, business owners aren't necessarily good at being lawyers, unless they have a legal practice. If they own a property or they are a farmer or they've got another professional business, you shouldn't expect that they're going to be good at putting legal documents together. What we need to do is have a plain English conversation. What the client needs is a plain English conversation with someone to understand what their real intent is.

Once that's achieved we effectively take it away in the back room with people who are good at this stuff, experts in fact, then that all gets done, all the legal documents get created. All the rest of the technical stuff gets done and we come back to the client with completed documents which effectively just need revision and signing, then everything is properly in place. The greatest misnomer is that most people think they've got to be involved in the whole process. That's not true. What the client needs to be involved in is just explaining what they want to happen and delegating the implementation and the documentation to the experts so that their time is not all chewed up.

The 90 Minute Exit Strategy Works For Anyone...

Susan: This is great Mark. Who does this apply to?

Mark: That's a great question Susan. Effectively the 90 Minute Exit Strategy could work for anyone. It could work for people who are just going about their day-to-day work, people who are employed. If you have people certainly from an estate planning point of view, it works for anyone, any business I know; it's exactly the same concept. It doesn't matter whether you have a motor dealership, you have a financial planning practice, you have a corner store that sells hot dogs. It really doesn't matter. The 90 Minute Strategy will work because it's a process that just helps to find out what it is you'd want to happen. And so the process is the same regardless of what business you happen to be in.

Once again because people seem to think this is such a complicated thing to do and they need to do it themselves, that's the key point. The reason people get stuck on this is because they think they need to do all the steps in the process themselves and they don't. By delegating and by outsourcing a number of steps in the strategy, the client's timeframe is very small.

And this applies to any business and people from all walks of life. It's exactly the same process.

What Happens When You Don't Have an Exit Strategy Sorted?

Susan: Very good. Can you give an example, Mark, of someone you know, going back to what you alluded to earlier, the 18% who don't get what they wanted? I'm curious if you could share an example of someone that didn't have this in place, respecting their privacy of course. To illustrate the downside of not having a plan in place?

Mark: Sure, absolutely. In fact, the story is of a close friend of mine. Though I tried to have a conversation with him on a number of occasions in regards to getting his exit strategy done, I could never convince him to attend to it, and as consequence nothing was done. I have a name for when this happens to folks, I call it the deferral dilemma. My friend is a perfect example of this. He just kept putting it off. He suffered what we in the business call the invincibility delusion. That feeling that it's always going to happen to the other guy and he doesn't need to pay attention to this because he's always going to be fine. It always happens to the other guy.

In today's modern world there are so many dangers that people face. There's also what we call the unaware[2] trapping. What that means is you just don't know what you don't know. He unfortunately hadn't paid attention to his exit strategy. He's one of the 95% that didn't have the right one in place. His wills weren't up to date and sadly he passed away in a plane accident. He left his family, his wife and his four children in a mess. He effectively left them destitute. They had to move out of their family home. The kids were in private schools and obviously that created a problem.

There's no money to pay for the kids' education anymore. The family's lives were ruined because this friend of mine hadn't taken the time to do proper planning. If you talk about 18% of the things he wanted to happen, probably only 5% of the things that he wanted to happen eventuated because he just hadn't taken 90 minutes effectively to sit down and talk about what he wanted so that I could have gone away and put a plan in place that would have created absolute certainty, confidence and security for his family, for the people that he loved and he cared for. He was a good guy, unfortunately in the end, he failed his family.

Susan: Once someone passes away there is no going back and fixing the mess, no turning back the clock to make things right for those they love. And without a proper plan, that's inevitably what happens I assume?

Mark: A lot of things can go wrong. He didn't have enough in place to leave sufficient assets to look after his family. That could have been fixed pretty easily. I have the saying that it's very important to ensure with your estate and your succession planning that the right money goes to the right people at the right time. One of the dangers if you don't pay attention to this is that part of your estate could mean that money goes to the children at the wrong ages and all of a sudden kids end up with too much money which they're in control of when they're still young and reckless. So it's not always a case of not having enough money.

That money can be flushed away and wasted or alternatively, money could end up all in the hands of the remaining spouse. If that person remarries there's always a risk that the next husband and their children could end up with a large slice of the estate which you intended for your own children. There's lots of dangers there. We don't want a situation where the legacy you intended for your own children, to leak to step children and so on. It happens all the time though.

Because not enough planning was done, the right money to the right people, at the right time is very important. You've got to make sure that what you leave to pay the kids' education goes for their education. What you leave to pay off the mortgage on the home, that's actually what happens to it. What you leave to make sure your family has an income stream, make sure that there are tools and capabilities in place and structures to make sure that if you've got someone who's very wasteful with money they're not wasting it at the expense of the other people in the family who need that money.

Susan: Your friend that passed away, why do you think he didn't have this in place? I'm assuming he was a successful business owner, so obviously he was a smart guy.

Mark: He was a successful business owner and financially at the time it was probably the worst financial time for him to pass in regard to their asset structures and so on. He suffered from the invincibility delusion and for his own reasons he just kept putting this off. We have another saying - the pompous presumption. In other words he avoided it when I would try to have a conversation, to sit him down to create an exit strategy. Pompously, he thought it was all taken care of because his accountant said things were okay.

Lawyers traditionally aren't proactive in this area either. Just because you've got a good lawyer and just because you've got a good accountant doesn't mean that this is all taken care of. When I would try to have conversations with him he would keep putting it off as he felt that this was something we could talk about in six months time when he had his new client signed up and the money was coming back in the door, he felt that would be a good time to handle it. A lot of people are waiting for the perfect time.

They keep waiting for their business to be perfectly established and perfectly profitable and when that's done they feel that will be the right time to do their estate and transition planning. There always seems to be that human frailty which is always searching for the perfect time to do this sort of work. In truth the perfect time is always now because you never know when the bus is going to come along and clean you up and then it's too late. Sadly people just keep deferring this because nobody wants to have a chat about what happens when you die.

It's not dinner table conversation. It's a conversation that's a little I guess not desirable, people put it off and they put it off. They always say we'll wait till John is finished with school. We'll wait till my business becomes more profitable or we'll wait until the kids are married. There's always an excuse as to why they want to wait to do this sort of planning.

There are Many Reasons to Have an Exit Plan in Place...

Importantly too, let's not just focus on what happens when people die, this also is needed when people are looking at selling their businesses, maybe they're coming up towards retirement age, they're looking at selling or transitioning their business to another partner. There a many different reasons to have an exit plan in place, not just for the unexpected exit.

Also people get so caught up in the business of running the business they don't take the time to look for someone who's going to buy the business at the right time, so they don't spend enough time early enough to put out feelers for people who might be interested in buying their business. They're not setting their business up to sell from a clinical point of view. And often they wait too long to sell and leave money on the table.

In short, they're not getting enough legal and tax advice to structure their business in such a way that it's an easy business to sell. Maybe they're not advertising the fact that they want to sell. They're not having enough conversations with people that are potential buyers and then the sad thing is what happens often times is people get to that age or that time in life where they want to sell their business and there's no market for it. They may be over a barrel, effectively because they only have one person who's interested in buying. They haven't set it up in such a way to maximize the profitability in those last few years, to maximize the value of the business.

You really need to look at having a three to five year plan in place to settle, to transition your business even if it's going to be one of your family members. Sadly once again people just seem to defer having those conversations and it comes back to people thinking there's too much work involved. They think it's too hard. They don't know where to start and that's a real key. People don't know where to start to do anything.

Why Having a Lawyer or CPA Doesn't Mean Your Plan Is Sound...

Susan: Hang on a second - coming back to your friend again, you said he thought he had taken care of everything? That's a bit disconcerting. I want to shine the light on that real quick. He had an accountant and a CPA and a lawyer? And still left his family destitute? How is that even possible?

Mark: He probably knew deep down he didn't have everything in place but it wasn't a conversation he wanted to have. He just didn't want to have the conversation because most people don't want to talk about death. Most people don't want to talk about dying and once again they don't know where to start. The thing with the accountants and the lawyers is that normally it's on the accountants tick list to have the conversation each year with the client and say, "You need to do X" as part of their compliance. They need to have the conversation with the client and say, "You need to review your will. You need to get your succession plan taken care of."

In my experience, it's mostly given lip service. In other words, they ask the question and they say something about it and then it's really the responsibility of the client to do something about it.

Which we know doesn't happen. Same with lawyers. Lawyers are very reactive people. Very few lawyers are proactive and so once again if a lawyer isn't given instruction they end up not doing anything. If you ask your lawyer to do a will they might send you a draft but then they tend not to follow up on a general basis.

There's always that need for a facilitator for someone to effectively run as a quarterback if you will, in the whole process to make sure all these things get done. You need to get your tactical team together and all the advisers need to be working together towards the same outcome. Finally, in regards to why my friend's business wasn't taken care of, it's probably because the other people may have mentioned that he needed to do it but he never allocated the time to get it done because he thought it was going to be too big a job.

In his mind it was too big an issue. It was going to take too long. He didn't realize that in 90 minutes we could have saved his family's financial life!

The Different Types of Exit Plans...

Susan: I'm sorry for your friend's family. Hopefully this book will prevent this from happening again. Let's talk about, for those of us that don't know what encompasses an exit strategy or an exit plan. Can you give us a 10,000 foot level view of what exactly that consists of?

Mark: Sure. There are two types of exit plans. One is voluntary and one is involuntary. The voluntary exit plan in broad terms is all about putting in place the structures and processes to set up your business for sale to find someone, to find the people that might be likely to buy it and to put in place the most cost effective, efficient and profitable structure from the buyers point of view. To make sure when they wish to exit their business, they get to have the right people in place who are ready to buy. The business is going to be profitable and they'll be able to sell it for the right amount of money. That money will transfer to the client in the most tax effective way, most efficient way for that client. That's voluntary exit planning.

Involuntary exit planning is the scenario where you get hit by the bus. In other words, you don't know when this is going to happen and to me this is always the most urgent one to get in place first, the involuntary exit plan. Getting the will, your power of attorney and your safe planning done, documented and in place. Once again that's the conversation people don't like having. They don't like thinking about the fact that they might die early. Statistically only 2% of people before the age of 65 know when they're going to die.

I'll say that again, 2% of people before the age of 65 know when they're going to die which means that the 98% of people that pass before the age of 65, their passing is absolutely unplanned, unrehearsed and they're unaware of the fact that it's about to happen to them. Those people, if they haven't got their succession planning in place, if they haven't documented their intent, then chances are they're going to be in a group of people where the efficiency of any documentation they may have, means there's about 99% chance of nothing happening at all.

The Only 3 Things You Need to Get Your Exit Plan in Place...

Mark: From a practical point of view Susan, there's only three things you need to get in place to make sure your exit plan, even your succession plan, your transition plan is going to give you what you want to happen. The first one is you need to have a conversation to identify and articulate what you want to happen. What's your intent? What's your desire? What are the outcomes that you'd wish for your family? For your business? You need to identify those and explain that to someone. Simple enough right? But most people resist this and are at great risk because of it.

The second piece to this is you need to ensure that you have a draft in simple English and you know who the key players are that you want to utilize.

The third step is to engage the appropriate tactical team who are specialists in their particular areas to document and help you fund the outcome you desire. You want to make sure you've identified your intent. Secondly you create something in simple English which the client understands and then make sure you've got a tactical team in place to ensure that is documented and funded. So what you want to happen, what your intent is, is what eventuates.

Here's Exactly How The 90 Minute Exit Strategy Works...

Susan: Very good and essentially this is what your 90 Minute Exit Strategy encompasses, correct?

Mark: That's it in a nutshell. Effectively we have initial conversations with people to make sure we can work together and so on, but that doesn't take long. The key things are we want to understand what people's intent is because whether people are doing this because they're planning to sell, to transition their business, whatever that might be we need to understand what your intent is. When do you want that to happen? How do you want to sell the business? Who do you want to sell it to? How much do you want to receive?

These are key things in regard to identifying your intent. The second thing is we need to get that down in simple English. The 80% theory that we talked about before, 80% is having a conversation with us understanding what your intent is and then writing it down on a piece of paper so that we can then engage the appropriate tactical team to then go away and document that to turn it into something which is legal. To make sure the funds are available so whether you're selling something or whether you pass away before your time, is there enough funds there to allow you to provide for your intent? In other words is your intent going to be honoured?

All the things you want for your family, the things you want for your business, will the money be there to ensure that they are realized? Those three simple steps are what we do in the 90 Minute Exit Strategy. We just identify what you want. We write it down in simple English and then we talk to you about the tactical team who will be engaged. Once that's done, you can go away and rest easy for a while and when the documentation is all completed and effectively that might take you a few more minutes to review, to sign and then you've got an exit plan in place that will honour your intent.

Whether you live, whether you pass, whether you're selling your business whatever the case is, you will have a plan in place that will ensure that what your intent is, is what happens.

The 90 Minute Exit Strategy Can Give You Peace of Mind...

Susan: Very good. I would imagine that's the peace of mind that people want when they started this in the first place.

Mark: Absolutely Susan, peace of mind is achieved when the client's desires are written. You just want to create peace of mind for the people that you care for. Probably if you don't want to create peace of mind for the people in your family then we can't help you. We can only help people who actually love and have passion for the people in their lives that are close to them.

The 90 Minute Exit Plan Works Even If You've Employed the Services of a CPA and Lawyer...

Susan: Right. Very good. Let me ask you this and thank you for that. If someone already has a lawyer, a CPA, does this program still work for them?

Mark: Absolutely Susan. That's a good question. What we find is that we have a checklist that we go through with people and that will help them identify if there are any issues. One of the things that I've found in the last 20 years of doing this sort of work, no matter how thorough people think they're taking care of things, there's always a few little holes that they may be missing in regard to their existing plan. What happens is if you're just dealing with your own accountant, your own lawyer, most people will have their own bent in regard to how they think you should structure your plan for you.

The advantage that we bring to the table is that I've dealt with lawyers and accountants throughout Australia over many years. That experience has taught me which questions to ask and which are the good questions to ensure that what you've got is taken care of. I've yet to find anybody that I've ever sat down with and had a conversation with where at the end of the day what they have in place covers all the bases that they would like covered. No matter what you've had done in the past, there may be some things that have changed in your life. There may be something that you didn't account for, that you're unaware of. Things that you didn't even know that you could do that are available for you to protect, to make sure as I said the right money goes to the right people at the right time.

More importantly most people who think they have this taken care of already, it's actually been a number of years since they've done their estate or their successional transition planning. Things change so quickly in life. There are opportunities they may not have been aware of when they did this in the first instance that are now available to them. It's a great opportunity for them to have a second opinion in regard to their existing structure. Tax law is changing all the time. Because of this, very few people have current up-to-date succession or transition plans in place.

Very few people have them but even those who do, a second opinion is usually invaluable because as I've yet to find anyone where we haven't been able to bring some things to their attention which would make their intent more in line with the outcome they're going to get.

Susan: This is exciting stuff. It can be complicated but I can see the beauty in simplifying like you have. It doesn't make it any less complex, but presenting it this way it's very appealing because like you said before, it's pretty overwhelming when we stop and think about handling this kind of stuff on our own.

Mark: Absolutely and that is the freezing point for 99% of the population. That is the reason that most people don't pay attention to the state of their succession planning, they think it's way too complicated. I like to bring simplicity into people's lives as well. The 90 Minute Exit Strategy is all about making it simple and having conversations in simple English with clients. Helping them understand that they don't need to understand the complexity in regards to putting these things together.

If I can have a conversation with someone and understand what their intent is and if I can write down in simple English what their ideal outcome is then really that's 80% of what needs to be done. All that can be done within 90 minutes and that puts them well on the path to getting all these issues sorted.

Here's Exactly How to Get Your Exit Plan in Place in Just 90 Minutes…

Susan: Very good. If someone wants to go through the 90 Minute Exit Strategy with you, how do they get in touch with you? What's the process?

Mark: The process is very simple. They visit our website at the90minuteexitstrategy.com or email me at team@the90minuteexitstrategy.com and we'll be happy to have an initial discussion with folks to see if we're in a position where we may be able to help them. From there we schedule the discovery session. It's all very easy.

Susan: Very good. Any last minute comments before we sign off?

Mark: Just in summary, exit strategy planning is really quite a simple thing and they shouldn't be put off by experiences they might have had in the past when they've had conversations with other professional advisors in regard to the complexities and difficulties that they espouse to you. In essence, within 90 minutes, we can have your exit strategy sorted once and for all.

Susan: Very exciting stuff Mark.

Mark: Thanks for helping Susan. I think it's an exciting process for us, helping people get this item that's been nagging them for years off their "to do" list so they can go off and enjoy life knowing they've sorted what matters.